DATE DUE

FEB 14 1996	
JAN 20 1996 NOV 14 1996	
JAN 21 1997	
NOV 2 9 1998	
SEP 0 5 1999	
9-19-99	
OCT 6	
MAR 2 3 2002	

DEMCO. INC. 38-2931

THIS IS
MAINE

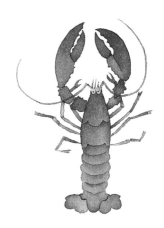

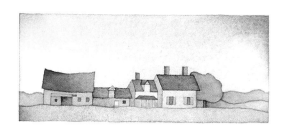

THIS IS
MAINE

by Margaret Blackstone

pictures by John Segal

Henry Holt and Company / New York

Henry Holt and Company, Inc.
Publishers since 1866
115 West 18th Street
New York, New York 10011

Henry Holt is a registered
trademark of Henry Holt and Company, Inc.

Published in Canada by Fitzhenry & Whiteside Ltd.,
195 Allstate Parkway, Markham, Ontario L3R 4T8.

Library of Congress Cataloging-in-Publication Data
Blackstone, Margaret.
This is Maine / by Margaret Blackstone : pictures by John Segal.
1. Maine—Juvenile literature.   I. Segal, John.   II. Title.
F19.3.B53   1995   974.1—dc20   94-12839

ISBN 0-8050-2800-5

First Edition—1995
Printed in the United States of America
on acid-free paper. ∞
1   3   5   7   9   10   8   6   4   2

The artist used watercolor and ink
to create the illustrations for this book.

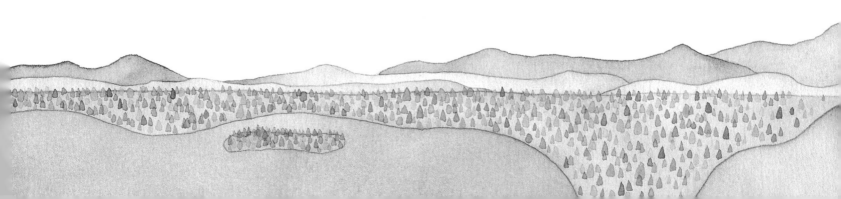

This is the rocky coast of Maine.

This is where Maine is on the map.

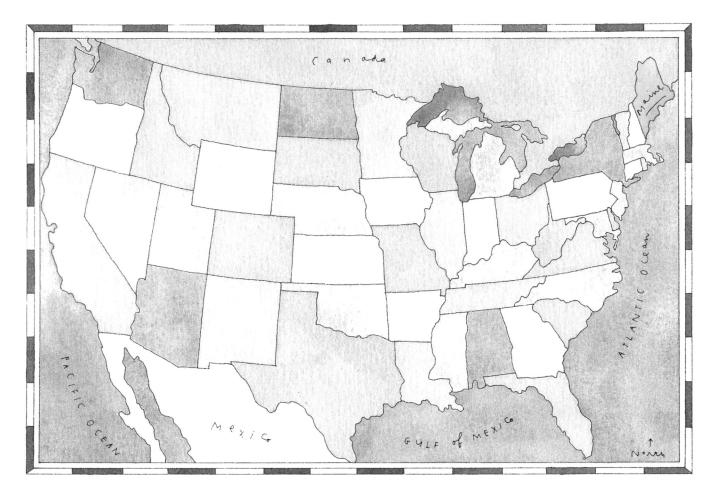

This is a lobster trap.

This is a
blueberry patch.

This is a good catch.

This is a rough sea.

This is a whitecap.

This is a clambake.

This is a tag sale.

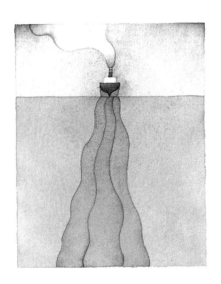

This is a boat's wake.

This is a humpback whale.

This is a seagull.

This is a one-clawed lobster, called a cull.

This is a seal feeling the sun

and eyeing a kite flying.

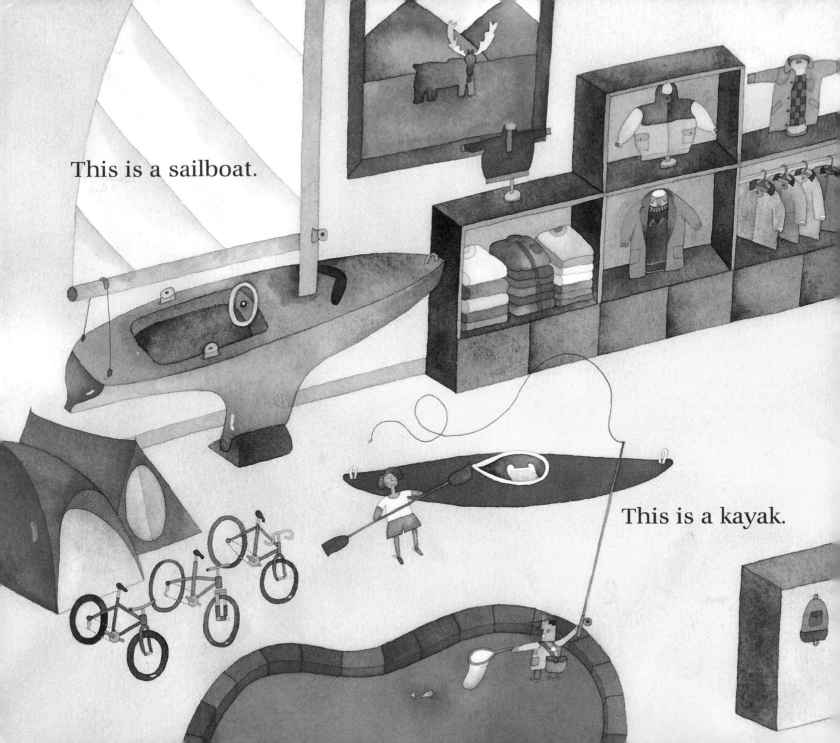

This is a sailboat.

This is a kayak.

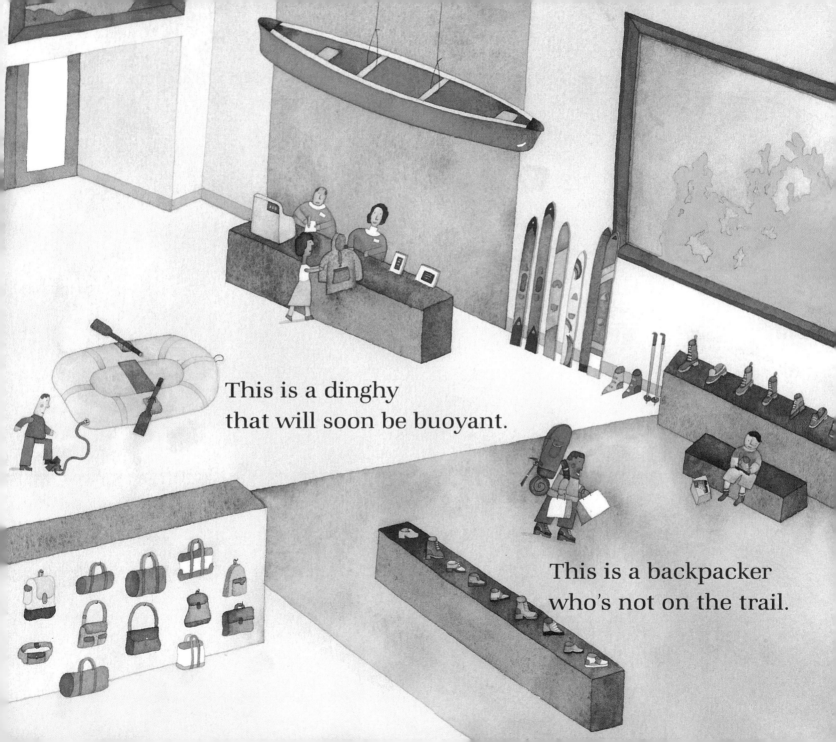

This is a dinghy
that will soon be buoyant.

This is a backpacker
who's not on the trail.

This is a lighthouse on an eastern point.

These are the fishermen mending their nets.

This is a hot spell.

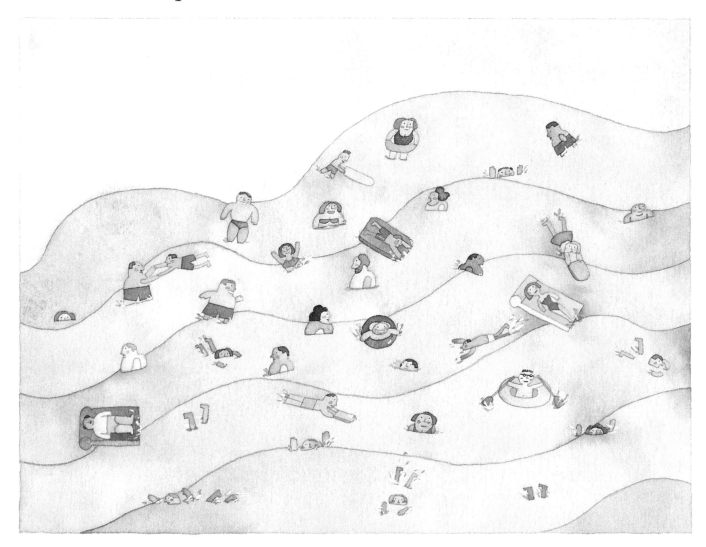

This is a sea swell.

This is how cold it gets in winter.

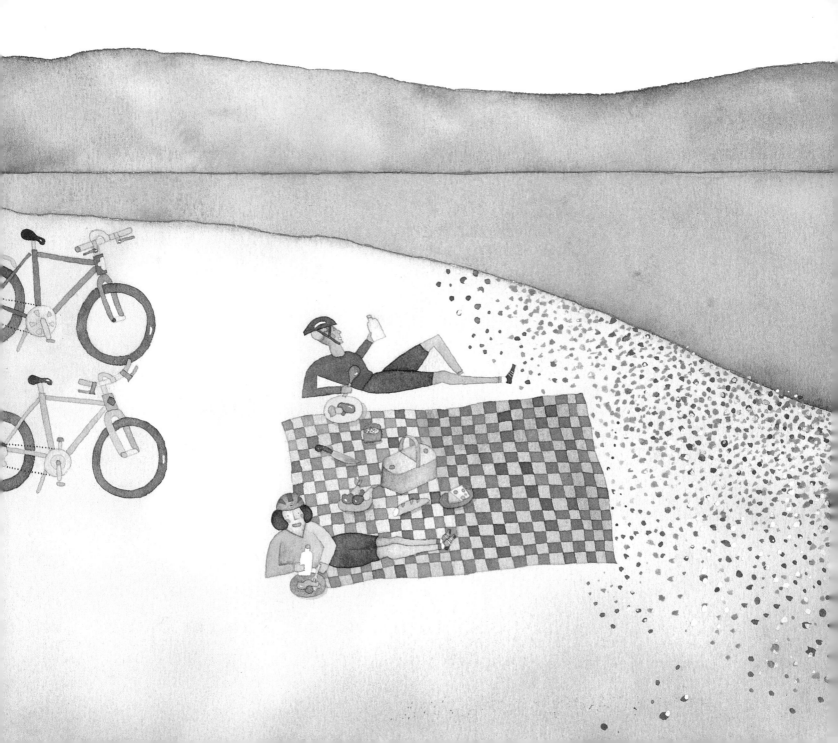

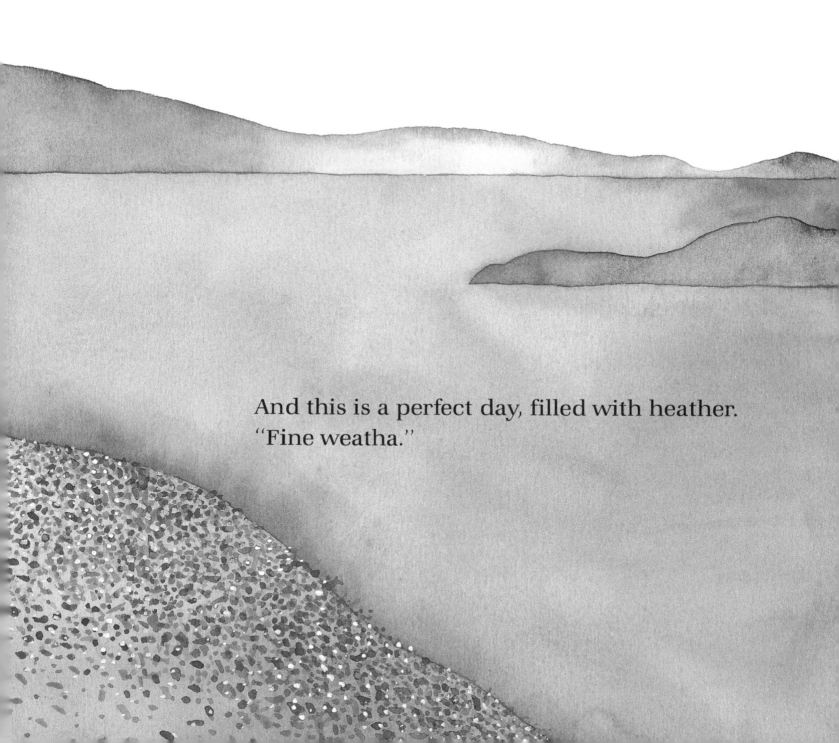

And this is a perfect day, filled with heather.
"Fine weatha."

This is a small skier,

and this is a big skier
shivering on the slope.
He let go of the rope tow.

This is a mountain.

This is a moose.

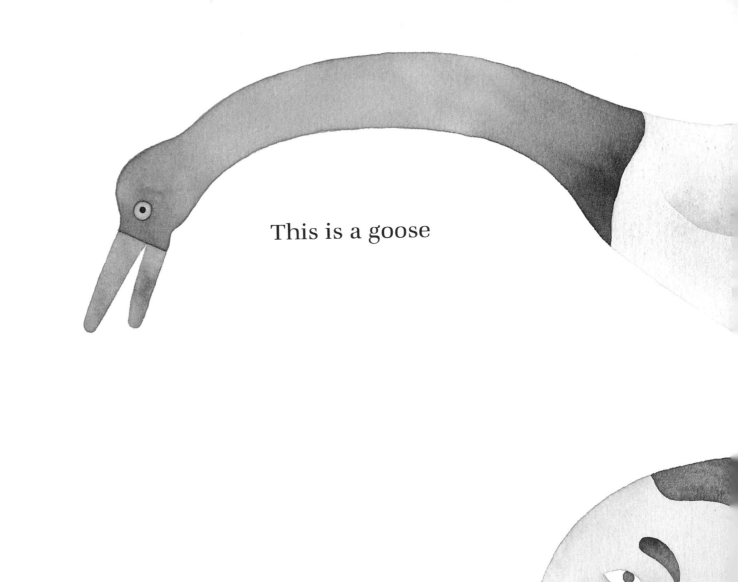

This is a goose

on a very odd roost.

This is a camp on a mountain lake
where kids swim and run races.

This is a tourist who looks like a tourist.

This is a Mainer who looks like a Mainer.

Mainers say
visitors are "from Away"
because for Mainers,
Maine is the only place.